CRUSHING OCD
WORKBOOK FOR KIDS

also by this author

The Grief Rock
A Book to Understand Grief and Love
Natasha Daniels
Illustrated by Lily Fossett
ISBN 978 1 83997 439 7
eISBN 978 1 83997 440 3

How to Parent Your Anxious Toddler
Natasha Daniels
ISBN 978 1 84905 738 7
eISBN 978 1 78450 148 8

of related interest

The Healthy Coping Colouring Book and Journal
Creative Activities to Help Manage Stress, Anxiety and Other Big Feelings
Pooky Knightsmith
Illustrated by Emily Hamilton
ISBN 978 1 78592 139 1
eISBN 978 1 78450 405 2

The A-Z Guide to Exposure
Creative ERP Activities for 75 Childhood Fears
Dawn Huebner, PhD and Erin Neely, PsyD
ISBN 978 1 83997 322 2
eISBN 978 1 83997 323 9

Can I tell you about OCD?
A guide for friends, family and professionals
Amita Jassi
Illustrated by Sarah Hull
ISBN 978 1 84905 381 5
eISBN 978 0 85700 736 0

CRUSHiNG OCD
WORKBOOK FOR KiDS

50 FUN ACTIVITIES TO OVERCOME OCD WITH CBT AND EXPOSURES

NATASHA DANIELS

ILLUSTRATED BY RICHY K. CHANDLER

Jessica Kingsley Publishers
London and Philadelphia

First published in Great Britain in 2024 by Jessica Kingsley Publishers
An imprint of John Murray Press

1

Copyright © Natasha Daniels 2024

The right of Natasha Daniels to be identified as the Author of the Work has been asserted by her in accordance with the Copyright, Designs and Patents Act 1988.

Front cover image source: Richy K. Chandler.

A CIP catalogue record for this title is available from the British Library and the Library of Congress

ISBN 978 1 83997 888 3
eISBN 978 1 83997 889 0

Printed and bound in the United States
by Integrated Books International

Jessica Kingsley Publishers' policy is to use papers that are natural, renewable and recyclable products and made from wood grown in sustainable forests. The logging and manufacturing processes are expected to conform to the environmental regulations of the country of origin.

Jessica Kingsley Publishers
Carmelite House
50 Victoria Embankment
London EC4Y 0DZ

www.jkp.com

John Murray Press
Part of Hodder & Stoughton Ltd
An Hachette Company

*To my three children, Chloe, Xander and Alex,
who have taught me more about how to
help kids than all of my schooling.*

CONTENTS

SECTION 4: OFFENSE
How to Bug OCD Back

63

SECTION 5: HOOKING OTHERS IN

81

SECTION 6: YOU ARE AWESOME!

91

SECTION 7: KEEPING UP YOUR SUCCESS

97

INTRODUCTION

FOR CAREGIVERS

Raising a child with OCD can be a challenge! It can be difficult to know how to support your child with these struggles. One of the best ways you can help your child is by giving them tools to help *themselves*.

Think of this workbook as a toolbox. I am going to fill your child's OCD toolbox one skill, one activity, at a time. By the end of this workbook, your child will have a full set of tools to crush their OCD. But just like any toolbox, it takes practice to become skilled at using these tools. As your child goes through this book, celebrate the small steps along the way. Small steps lead to big changes over time.

This book is meant to be digested in sequential order. The activities build upon each other. It is helpful that you do the activities in the order they are presented and avoid skipping around. Depending on your child's age, you might do the workbook together. I recommend taking your time going through the activities and allowing space to practice the concepts as they are learned.

This workbook is for educational purposes only and is not intended to replace the guidance of a qualified professional. Ideally, you will use this workbook in conjunction with a child OCD therapist who does ERP therapy (Exposure Response Prevention). It is also important that you build your own toolbox to better support your child. OCD is a family affair, and we all need to know our part. I have included caregiver resources at the end of this book for ongoing support.

FOR THERAPISTS

This workbook can offer a convenient and effective way to build skills and knowledge in between therapy sessions. As you move from OCD education to skill building, you'll find activities that will complement your therapeutic work and hardwire the approaches you are teaching each step of the way.

SECTION ONE
UNDERSTANDING OCD AND ITS MANY DISGUISES

Do you know we have over 6000 thoughts a day? Can you imagine that? That is a **lot** of thoughts. These thoughts usually come in and out of our awareness all day long. We barely notice any of these thoughts. They come in...they get filtered out.

But when you have OCD, the gears that filter those thoughts jam up. Thoughts that should easily go through the filter get stuck. When thoughts get stuck, the whole system gets confused. Your mind starts to **notice** these thoughts. It then starts to **examine** these thoughts. It starts to give **meaning** to thoughts that should have been just filtered away.

Her shirt is pretty

Do I have to pee?

What will I have for lunch?

I wish this class would end

The worst part is that when you focus on these thoughts, **more** of them start to appear. These are called **intrusive thoughts** because, like an intruder, these thoughts are unwanted.

Everyone with OCD has the same filtering issue, but the thoughts that get stuck are different for each person.

OCD is like ice cream. There are lots of different flavors, but at the end of the day, they're all cold and they all melt. OCD has lots of different themes

(we'll talk more about that later), but it's all the same OCD problem: stuck gears and a jammed filter.

Did you know that OCD is pretty common? In fact, one out of every 200 kids has OCD—that is about the same as kids with diabetes. That means it is highly likely that you know someone with OCD and are not even aware of it!

Even though no one wants a jammed filter, people with OCD tend to have some pretty cool superpowers as well. People with OCD are often deep thinkers; they may notice things other people do not. This helps them be super creative, with a talent for coming up with new ideas and creations!

They also tend to be kind-hearted and thoughtful. They are aware of people's emotions and can care deeply about others. Those are powerful skills to have!

So the goal is to help unjam your filter so you can have those amazing superpowers without all the struggle of OCD.

Before we learn how to crush OCD and unjam that filter, let's start by celebrating your superpowers!

ACTIVITY 1
FIRST LET'S CELEBRATE YOUR SUPERPOWERS

We are going to spend **a lot** of time learning how to crush your OCD, but before we dive into that, it is important to celebrate the parts of you that are amazing! Let's figure out what those are for you!

DIRECTIONS

Think about what types of superpowers you have. This can be anything from skills like Lego building to personality traits like being considerate or kind.

EXTRA TIP

Not sure what your superpowers are? Take a survey. Ask the people who know you best what they think your amazing qualities might be!

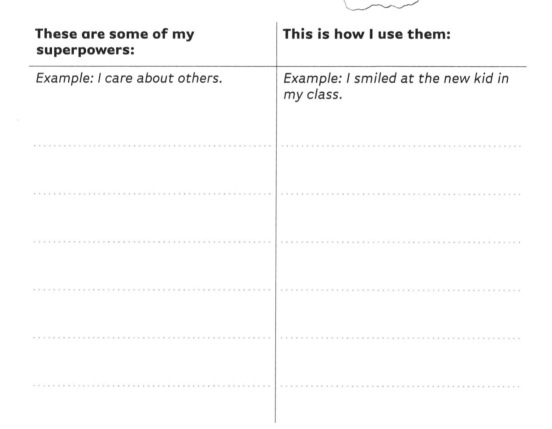

These are some of my superpowers:	This is how I use them:
Example: I care about others.	*Example: I smiled at the new kid in my class.*

CRUSHING OCD WORKBOOK FOR KIDS

ACTIVITY 2
WHAT IS JAMMING YOUR FILTER RIGHT NOW?

Let's discuss what intrusive OCD thoughts are jamming your filter right now. Remember, OCD thoughts change over time, so this is just a snapshot of what is going on lately.

DIRECTIONS
Think about the intrusive OCD thoughts that jam up and get stuck most often. Write them down below.

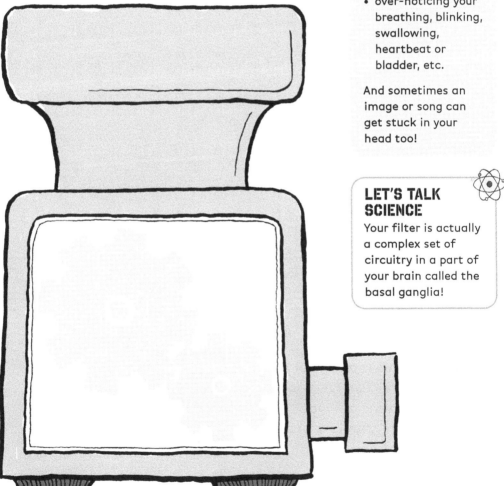

EXTRA TIP
Sometimes people have jammed **feelings**, not thoughts. Here are a few OCD feelings that can get jammed:

- feeling grossed out
- feeling things are not complete
- feeling things aren't "just right"
- over-noticing your breathing, blinking, swallowing, heartbeat or bladder, etc.

And sometimes an image or song can get stuck in your head too!

LET'S TALK SCIENCE
Your filter is actually a complex set of circuitry in a part of your brain called the basal ganglia!

UNDERSTANDING YOUR CORE FEAR (OR FEELING)

You can have a zillion different intrusive OCD thoughts or feelings that get jammed in your filter. But typically you only have a few core fears (or feelings). That means your filter gets stuck on certain thoughts, but they all have similar core fears.

Let's take a look at this in action.

These are just a few examples. Everyone will have different thoughts and core fears. Even if you have similar thoughts to those below, your core fear might be completely different.

DIRECTIONS

Now that you understand how intrusive thoughts can have one core fear, let's discover what that might be for you! Take one intrusive thought and answer the questions.

EXTRA TIP

Most people have a few core fears, so it's okay if you have more than one. Also, make sure you go all the way down the rabbit hole and keep asking, "What's the worst thing that can happen if...?" to make sure you get to the bottom of the core fear.

What is one of your intrusive OCD thoughts that gets jammed?
Example: That object might be full of germs.

....

What does your OCD say is the worst thing that
can happen because of that?
Example: I might get germs on me if I touch that.

....

What is the worst thing that can happen because of that?
Example: I might get sick.

....

What is the worst thing that can happen because of that?
Example: I might throw up.

....

What is the core fear?
Example: Fear of throwing up.

....

REAL-LIFE PRACTICE

Pay attention to what your OCD thoughts are telling you for
the next few days. Take out a sheet of paper and jot them
down. For each thought, go through this exercise. Remember to go all
the way down the rabbit hole. Come back here and write down your most
common core fears.

My most common core fears are:

1. ....

2. ....

3. ....

WHAT ARE YOUR OCD FLAVORS RIGHT NOW?

Did you learn some of your core fears? Often OCD core fears are called OCD themes or subtypes. This is just a fancy way of saying the different types of OCD flavors you are dealing with at the moment! Remember, flavors (OCD themes) can change over time. It can help to understand the many disguises that OCD might wear, even if you don't struggle with some of these themes. Most people have just a handful of themes at any given time.

DIRECTIONS
Here are some examples of the most common OCD themes. Read each description and check the box if that OCD theme sounds like your OCD. Don't see your theme? Fill in an empty bucket with your OCD theme!

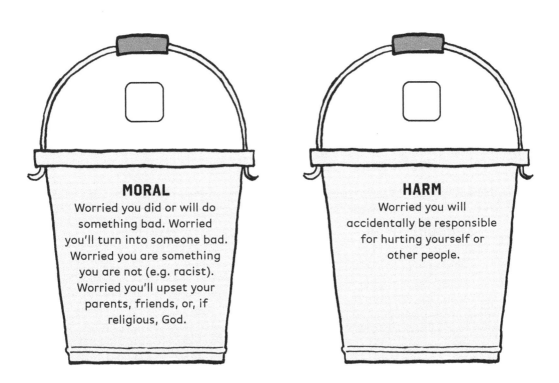

MORAL
Worried you did or will do something bad. Worried you'll turn into someone bad. Worried you are something you are not (e.g. racist). Worried you'll upset your parents, friends, or, if religious, God.

HARM
Worried you will accidentally be responsible for hurting yourself or other people.

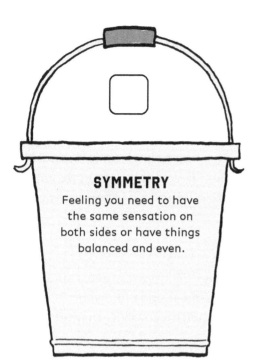

SYMMETRY
Feeling you need to have the same sensation on both sides or have things balanced and even.

CONTAMINATION
The fear that something (or someone) has something on it that you don't like or causes you anxiety or feelings of disgust. Usually, this can spread to other things or people that you then try to avoid.

SENSORIMOTOR
Being super focused on something happening in your body. This can be your blinking, your breathing, your need to pee or poop, your heart beating, your swallowing or any other bodily sensation.

JUST RIGHT
Feeling that something doesn't feel "just right" or is incomplete so you need to repeat it. This can be words, sounds, things you see or read as well as things you do, like brushing your teeth or wiping after using the bathroom.

IMAGES OR SONGS

An image or song gets stuck in your head, and you get worried it will never go away.

EXISTENTIAL

This is a big word for big questions. You worry about tons of things like what is the purpose of life? What if we aren't real? How can we be so small in a universe so big?

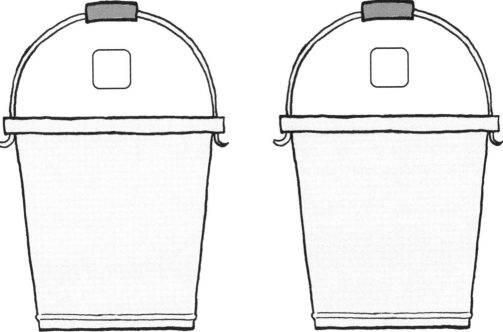

Let's Give OCD a Name!

Now that you have a really good understanding of your intrusive thoughts, core fears and even your main OCD themes, let's make things super simple. Let's give OCD a name. Naming your OCD does a few powerful things.

First, it reminds you that **you are not your OCD**. It is a filtering issue. When you name your OCD, you separate it from who you truly are. In fact, the things that get stuck in your filter the most are usually things that are the complete opposite of who you are or what you believe.

Second, it makes it more fun! OCD is hard, and when we poke fun and give it a silly name, you take your power back. Even some teens and adults name their OCD!

To make this idea stick, we'll be calling OCD **Mr. O** from now on in this workbook.

EXTRA TIP

Need some inspiration? Think of a funny name, a name that relates to your OCD themes or a name that relates to a character you don't like. Here are some examples: Mr. O (for OCD), Bob (giving it a real name can be funny), Mr. Doubt, Ms. Germy, Ms. JustRight, Mr. OhNo!

DIRECTIONS
In the frame, draw what your OCD will look like and give it a name!

REAL-LIFE PRACTICE
Tell your parents what your OCD name is. Instead of using "OCD," use the new name. For example, you can say, "Mr. O is bothering me right now."

MY NAME IS:

HOW MR. O GETS FED (COMPULSIONS)

Mr. O (that's what we'll be calling OCD from now on) grows bigger when you "feed" him. First Mr. O gives you an intrusive thought or feeling. Then he demands that you do or avoid something to get relief from that thought or feeling. The problem is...the more you do or avoid, the bigger Mr. O grows!

These things you do (or avoid) are called compulsions. When you do compulsions, you create a loop that grows more intrusive thoughts over time and makes Mr. O even bigger.

5. Repeats over and over

1. You have an intrusive thought or feeling

2. You do what Mr. O wants

4. Mr. O gets stronger and bothers you even more

3. You feed Mr. O

DIRECTIONS

Compulsions (Mr. O's food) can be so many things. The first step in shrinking Mr. O is figuring out what you do to feed him!

Even though everyone with OCD has an OCD loop they get stuck in, everyone's loops look different. Let's see how one of your loops works!

1. My intrusive thought:

. . . .

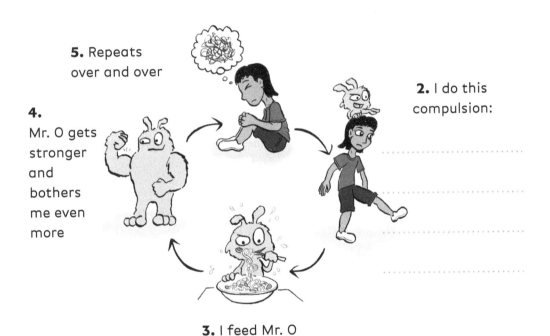

5. Repeats over and over

4. Mr. O gets stronger and bothers me even more

2. I do this compulsion:

. . . .

. . . .

. . . .

3. I feed Mr. O

LET'S TALK SCIENCE
We are using Mr. O and food as a metaphor, but there is actual science behind this. When you do compulsions, you are growing the neural pathways in your brain that make OCD stronger.

WHAT MR. O TELLS YOU TO DO (PHYSICAL COMPULSIONS)

It is important to understand the many ways Mr. O will get you to feed him. He can be very sneaky and try all sorts of creative ways to get you to grow him. Let's talk about some of the many ways Mr. O can boss you into feeding him. These include:

- washing
- checking
- asking questions
- counting
- tapping
- researching
- overdoing something
- doing something a certain way
- repeatedly doing something
- saying something a certain way
- confessing.

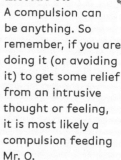

EXTRA TIP

A compulsion can be anything. So remember, if you are doing it (or avoiding it) to get some relief from an intrusive thought or feeling, it is most likely a compulsion feeding Mr. O.

Those are just a few behaviors (called physical compulsions) that grow Mr. O. But there is a big compulsion that people often miss... avoidance! Mr. O is often bossy, but sometimes he'll tell you to avoid something. Here are a few examples of how Mr. O might use avoidance as a compulsion:

- avoid objects, people or places
- avoid saying certain words
- avoid sitting in certain spots
- avoid wearing certain clothes
- avoid eating certain foods.

DIRECTIONS

Let's figure out when you are feeding Mr. O. In the first column, write down your most common intrusive thoughts or feelings. Be as specific as you can. In the second column, write down all the things you do or avoid (compulsions) to make those intrusive thoughts go away.

Intrusive thoughts/feelings:	Compulsions I do when I have that thought/feeling:

ACTIVITY 8
WHAT MR. O TELLS YOU TO THINK (MENTAL COMPULSIONS)

Mr. O can change the way he gets you to feed him. He might have you do things, ask things or avoid things. But he might also have you **think** things. This is a sneaky move because no one else will notice what is going on. That is why it is so important for you to realize that only you have the full power to squash Mr. O and make him smaller. You are the only one who knows everything Mr. O is having you do (or avoid) to grow him bigger.

Mental compulsions are things Mr. O wants you to do in your head. Many kids don't realize that these mental games they do for Mr. O are compulsions that will grow him just as fast as physical compulsions.

Here are just a few examples of what mental compulsions can look like:

- arguing and debating with OCD
- trying to prove OCD wrong
- counting in your head
- saying certain phrases
- trying to "undo" a bad thought by:
  - praying
  - saying a certain phrase
  - mentally erasing it
- doing mental games like adding or counting letters or numbers.

EXTRA TIP

A mental compulsion can be anything. So remember, if you are doing it to get some relief from an intrusive thought or feeling, it is most likely a mental compulsion feeding Mr. O.

Not everyone will have both physical and mental compulsions, but it is good to be aware of what they are in case they pop up. Mr. O doesn't play by the rules, and he changes his tactics often. So the more you know about his moves, the better you'll be able to overcome them!

DIRECTIONS

Let's figure out if you are feeding Mr. O with mental compulsions. In the first column, write down your most common intrusive thoughts or feelings. Be as specific as you can. In the second column, write down any things you might do in your mind to make those intrusive thoughts go away.

Intrusive thoughts/feelings:	Mental compulsions I do after that thought:

ACTIVITY 9
WHAT MR. O TELLS YOUR FAMILY TO DO (ACCOMMODATIONS)

Mr. O is no fool! He knows that he will be fed more often if he involves the people who love and care about you. He also knows it can be really hard for family members not to give in to Mr. O as well.

When family members help you complete an OCD loop, it is called an accommodation. Accommodations are things your loved ones do to help you complete your loop. Often Mr. O will get you to nag, beg and bother your family to do the things Mr. O demands.

Let's look at a few examples of accommodations that grow Mr. O:

- answering reassurance questions
- responding to confessions with reassurance
- answering repeated questions about your health
- answering repeated questions about you getting sick
- answering questions about food, expiration dates and safety
- answering the way Mr. O wants them to respond
- repeating things for Mr. O
- doing things that Mr. O won't let you do
- helping you carry out a compulsion
- touching things for you
- following the specific rules Mr. O demands
- washing or wiping things down for you
- avoiding certain words, places or things.

That's just a few!

DIRECTIONS

Let's figure out what loved ones are doing to accommodate and grow Mr. O. In the first column, write down your most common intrusive thoughts or feelings. Be as specific as you can. In the second column, write down all the things Mr. O wants your loved ones to do.

EXTRA TIP

An accommodation can be anything. So remember, if your family is doing it because Mr. O is demanding it, it is most likely an OCD accommodation.

CRUSHING OCD WORKBOOK FOR KIDS

Intrusive thoughts/feelings:	Accommodations Mr. O wants others to do:

REAL-LIFE PRACTICE

For the next week, pay attention to what things Mr. O is telling you to do, avoid or have others do. Come back to the lists above and add the new things you notice!

MR. O ROBS YOU OF THESE THINGS (VALUES)

Mr. O isn't just annoying. He can rob you of time and try to ruin things you love. It can be helpful to look at what things you want to take back from OCD.

Here are some of the things Mr. O can rob from you:

- **Time:** Mr. O can take time away from your life when you could be doing something else.
- **Self-esteem:** Mr. O can make you feel bad about yourself.
- **Activities:** Mr. O can make it hard to do or complete activities that you enjoy.
- **Social life:** Mr. O can make it hard to socialize with friends.
- **Family:** Mr. O can cause arguments with people you care about.
- **Focus:** Mr. O can make it hard to focus on anything but him.
- **Belongings:** Mr. O can take the objects, toys and items you love and make them hard to use.

These are just a few examples. Let's explore what Mr. O is taking from you that you want back!

DIRECTIONS
Use the list above as a guide to think about what things Mr. O is taking away from you. Write down the things you want to take back from OCD as you learn to squish him and make him super tiny! Also think about **why** these things matter to you and jot that down as well.

SECTION TWO
LET'S TALK ABOUT
MR. O

An important part of crushing Mr. O is being able to talk about him. Mr. O is very good at sabotaging this! In this section, you'll uncover the many ways Mr. O might make it hard to discuss OCD. You'll also come up with a plan for how to talk about him without feeding him.

WE DON'T TALK ABOUT MR. O!

Mr. O's first move is to make it hard for you to talk about OCD with other people. If you can't talk about him, you can't come up with a plan to shrink him! Let's change that!

Here are some reasons Mr. O might tell you not to talk about OCD with anyone:

- It's embarrassing.
- You feel weird.
- You feel different.
- You think if they know, they'll make you face your fears.
- You think they won't understand.
- You think you are the only one with these thoughts.
- You think if you talk about OCD, it will make it worse.

Now it's your turn!

DIRECTIONS
Write down some of the reasons you feel uncomfortable talking about Mr. O.

REAL-LIFE PRACTICE
Do you know that a ton of famous people have OCD? It's true! Get a caregiver to help you do an internet search on famous people with OCD. See if there is anyone you know!

Beating MR. O at His Own Game

In the last activity, you listed all the reasons Mr. O makes it hard for you to talk about OCD. Let's discover reasons why those things aren't true!

DIRECTIONS

In the first column, write down the reasons you listed in Activity 11. In the second column, list the reasons why it is not true.

EXTRA TIP

Not sure why those thoughts aren't true? Ask a caregiver or your therapist to go through the reasons with you!

Mr. O tells me *not* to talk about OCD because:	I shouldn't listen to him because:

HOW WE TALK ABOUT MR. O

It can be helpful to come up with a plan for how you'll talk about Mr. O. When you do this, Mr. O has less of a chance of keeping you quiet.

DIRECTIONS
Fill in your answers below.

We decided to call OCD:

I'm comfortable talking to these people about OCD:

When OCD is bothering me my caregiver can say:

EXTRA TIP

Mr. O might want you to keep your OCD super private. It is okay to have privacy and not tell friends or family that you don't see often, but it is helpful for everyone in your home to know at least a little about your OCD. After all, OCD is a family affair, and Mr. O will involve everyone in your family in some way.

I prefer that these people don't know about my OCD:

I prefer that these people don't know about these particular OCD themes/worries:

WHEN WE TALK ABOUT MR. O

It can be helpful to create a plan for when you'll talk about Mr. O. Mr. O will want to talk to those around you so that he'll get fed. Make sure when you are talking about OCD, it is for **you** and not because Mr. O wants reassurance. A good way to prevent this from happening is to have your caregiver be the one to decide when to talk about Mr. O.

Avoid planning to talk at a specific time each day, as Mr. O will put it on his calendar and turn it into a compulsion session.

DIRECTIONS
Fill in your answers below.

I want this person to check in with me about my OCD:

. . . .

I would find it helpful to talk . . . . times per day

or . . . . times per week about Mr. O.

These are the general times I would be most open to talking about Mr. O. Circle answer(s):

    Mornings   After school   Weekends   Evening   Before bed

These are the things I would want to talk about:

. . . .

. . . .

My caregiver will be the one to bring up the conversation. If I don't want to talk about it at that time, I'll say:

. . . .

If I want to talk about OCD, I'll ask my caregiver if we can talk. I'll know if it is Mr. O trying to get fed if these are the type of questions or topics he wants to discuss:

....

....

....

....

SECTION THREE
DEFENSE
WHAT TO DO WHEN OCD IS KNOCKING

ow that you understand how Mr. O bothers you and how he gets you to grow him bigger, it's time to build up your ninja skills!

There are two ways you are going to crush Mr. O and both are equally important.

First, you are going to play **defense**. This is how you **respond** to Mr. O when he comes knocking. This is what you do when you are getting OCD thoughts and feelings.

You can't stop Mr. O from giving you upsetting thoughts and feelings, but you can choose what you do with them. Every time Mr. O wants you to do (or avoid) something, you get to decide what **your** move will be.

In this section, I'll go over all the different powerful defense moves you can use when Mr. O comes knocking.

Let's dive in!

I SPY WITH MY LITTLE EYE, MR. O
LEVEL 1: NOTICE

You can think of these defense tools as ninja moves. Some deliver a powerful punch and others are enough to just give Mr. O a push back.

I'll talk about each ninja move in order of how powerful they are. But remember, any ninja move is better than no ninja moves at all.

EXTRA TIP
Level 1 is just noticing the compulsions, not trying to resist doing them.

The first basic ninja move is noticing when Mr. O wants you to do something. Often OCD is so sneaky it will make doing compulsions a habit. You might be used to giving Mr. O what he wants to make him go away. You can't conquer something if you don't know when it is creeping up on you.

In Level 1, you'll notice when it's Mr. O. This will build your awareness of what things you do or avoid to grow OCD. This is a powerful first step in making OCD smaller.

DIRECTIONS

For the next three days, notice when Mr. O wants you (or those around you) to do or avoid something because of OCD thoughts and feelings. Keep a record of them in the following table.

Date:	OCD thought/feeling:	OCD compulsion:

You can WaiT, MR. O

LEVEL 2: DELAY

With Level 1 under your belt, you are picking up some strength! Now for the next ninja move – delaying. It might be hard to not give Mr. O what he wants, but you can make him wait! Delaying, Level 2, teaches you how to handle the uncomfortable feelings OCD throws at you for a period of time.

Here are some examples of what delaying a compulsion might look like:

- delay washing your hands
- delay asking your loved one that OCD reassurance question
- delay confessing a thought
- delay counting
- delay making something even or balanced
- delay redoing something
- delay checking
- delay doing that mental game
- delay moving away from something or someone.

Those are just a few examples!

DIRECTIONS

What compulsions do you think you can delay? Remember any small step is better than no step at all! Write down what compulsions you will try to delay for the next week. Pick a specific amount of time you will try to delay doing the compulsion.

LET'S TALK SCIENCE

Delaying is actually having an impact on the mechanisms inside your brain! When you delay giving into a compulsion, you slow down the firing of neural pathways. Think about it as a traffic stop in the middle of a neural highway. The more often you do that, the weaker those neural pathways become.

I will try to delay these compulsions:	I will try to delay it for this amount of time:
....	....
....	....
....	....
....	....
....	....
....	....
....	....
....	....
....	....
....	....
....	....
....	....

REAL-LIFE PRACTICE

If you are able to delay the compulsion for your targeted time, ask yourself if you can delay it even longer. Can you set a best score each day that you try to beat? Make doing this an ongoing practice!

I'M NOT LISTENING, MR. O

LEVEL 3: IGNORE

An advanced ninja skill is the art of Level 3: ignoring Mr. O. When you don't listen to OCD and resist giving in to the compulsions, you make him smaller! The more you resist, the more he shrinks.

Here are some examples of what ignoring a compulsion might look like:

- not asking for reassurance
- not washing your hands
- not repeating things
- not checking
- not counting
- not avoiding
- not balancing/evening out
- not mentally debating or arguing with OCD
- not saying particular phrases
- not demanding others do things in a specific way.

Those are just a few examples!

DIRECTIONS

What compulsions do you think you can ignore? Remember any small step is better than no step at all! Write down what compulsions you will try to ignore. You can start with something very small to get your feet wet.

LET'S TALK SCIENCE

When you ignore OCD, you are impacting the mechanisms inside your brain! When you don't give in to a compulsion, you don't fire those neural pathways. Think about a road that no one uses. The more often you do that, the smaller those neural pathways become. You can turn a six-lane neural highway into a bumpy country road, making OCD weaker.

I will try to ignore these compulsions:

....

....

....

....

REAL-LIFE PRACTICE

If you can ignore the compulsions you picked, try to maintain your progress by permanently ignoring those compulsions! The more you can resist, the smaller Mr. O will get.

HOW ABOUT THiS, MR. O?

LEVEL 4: DOING THE OPPOSITE

Your most powerful defense move is Level 4: doing the opposite. OCD is bossy and demanding. So you are extra powerful when you not only ignore what he is saying but do the complete opposite! This is a strong and brave ninja move to make.

Don't worry. Even if that seems impossibly hard right now, all your practice with the other ninja levels will build up your skills for this advanced move.

There are a few OCD themes that may not have an opposite and that's okay. You'll make even more powerful moves in Section Four when we talk about offense.

So what would doing the opposite look like for some OCD flavors? Here are just a few examples below from various OCD themes:

- Make things feel imbalanced.
- Make things messy or imperfect on purpose.
- Touch something OCD says not to touch.
- Say something OCD says not to say.
- Do something OCD says not to do.
- Sarcastically tell OCD you might be what OCD says you'll become.
- Sarcastically tell OCD you might do what he says you might do.

DIRECTIONS

What compulsions do you think have an opposite you can do? Write down some compulsions and the opposite you will try to do for the next week. Try to do the opposite every time you get the urge to do the compulsion. Over time it will get easier!

Compulsion:	Opposite behavior I will do:

REAL-LIFE PRACTICE

If you are able to do the opposite for some compulsions, see if you can do it permanently. The more you do the opposite of what OCD wants, the smaller he becomes!

Play The OCD Game With Levels

Now that you know all the ninja levels, let's talk about how to use them every day! You can do this by playing the OCD Game. The OCD Game is simple:

1. Mr. O comes knocking.
2. You recognize that it is Mr. O. (Level 1)
3. You see what Mr. O wants you to do or avoid.
4. You pick a ninja move level you can do in that moment.
   - Can you delay the compulsion? (Level 2)
   - Can you ignore the compulsion? (Level 3)
   - Can you do the opposite of the compulsion? (Level 4)
5. Carry out your ninja move!
6. Are you done or can you follow up with a higher ninja level?

You won't always feel strong enough to do a Level 3 or 4, but even a Level 1 or 2 is showing up and playing the OCD Game. Any move in the right direction will help! When you don't show up and play the OCD Game, Mr. O automatically wins.

DIRECTIONS

Let's make a comic strip story about you playing the OCD Game. In Box 1 draw Mr. O giving you a thought. In Box 2 draw you recognizing it's Mr. O. In Box 3 draw Mr. O telling you what to do or avoid. In Box 4 pick a level and draw a picture doing it. In Box 5 draw a picture of you doing your ninja move! In Box 6 draw a picture of you picking another ninja move!

Remembering Your Ninja Moves

Ninja moves are great, but only if you remember to do them! Mr. O is loud, and his demands might make you lose focus on all the powerful moves you are learning. To help with that, let's find ways you can remember to play the OCD Game throughout your day.

DIRECTIONS

It can be helpful to remind yourself of your ninja OCD levels. Think of places where you can put reminders. What can your reminder look like? Below is an example. Get a piece of paper out and make your own reminders. Then put them in places you'll see around your house.

Level 1: Realize it is Mr. O

Level 2: Delay compulsion

Level 3: Ignore compulsion

Level 4: Do the opposite

OTHER NINJA FIGHTERS TO SUPPORT YOU

You are not in this alone. You have people around you who love and support you. They can help you with your defense ninja moves and the OCD Game. What do you want them to say if they see you doing a compulsion that doesn't involve them? We are going to spend a whole section of this workbook talking about when Mr. O **does** involve them, so we'll skip that part for now.

Loved ones can help you in many ways including:

- noticing when it is OCD
- reminding you to pick a level
- motivating you to do a level by offering bravery points to get prizes and privileges
- letting you deal with this yourself.

It is helpful for the people around you to know how you want them to support you.

DIRECTIONS
Come up with ways you want your loved ones to respond when they see Mr. O bothering you. Pick one of the options listed above or make up your own. You might want different people to respond in different ways. Write down all the important people around you and how you want each one of them to respond.

REAL-LIFE PRACTICE

Have a family meeting or meet with each person alone and discuss this plan with them.

Person:

When I'm struggling with OCD, you can help by:

Person:

When I'm struggling with OCD, you can help by:

Person:

When I'm struggling with OCD, you can help by:

DON'T LET MR. O OUTSMART YOUR DEFENSE!

Mr. O is not easily outsmarted. In fact, he will take your ninja defense moves and try to make his countermove. But you can stay one step ahead by being aware of the type of things Mr. O might do.

DIRECTIONS

Below are some ways Mr. O can try to outsmart you in the OCD Game. In what ways do you think Mr. O will try to stop you? When you think about how Mr. O will try to outsmart you, you'll be one step ahead and will be less likely to fall for his tricks!

- Tell you it's too hard to do any level.
- Convince you to do the compulsion just in case.
- Make you think you believe the things you sarcastically agree with when talking back.
- Tell you there are no small steps you can take.
- Get mad at others when they try to help you.

Mr. O might try to outsmart me by doing these things:	I'll outsmart him by doing this:

TALKING BACK TO MR. O

Mr. O wants you to talk to him. He wants you to argue with him. He loves a good debate. But you can beat him at his own game. You can talk to Mr. O, but not in the way he wants! If Mr. O is telling you something upsetting, you can sarcastically agree with him. That makes his head spin, and he doesn't know what to do with that!

Here are some examples:

- Yes, Mr. O, I may or may not get sick!
- Yup, I might do that.
- It's true, I might turn into that.
- You never know, that may or may not happen!
- You're right, I might think that.
- You're right, this feeling may or may not ever go away.

EXTRA TIP
This is a powerful ninja kick to Mr. O's plan. Remember, just because you sarcastically agree with Mr. O doesn't mean you think those things or you are those things. You are just outsmarting him at his own game! Also, make sure not to say the exact same thing each time. Mr. O can turn even that into a compulsion!

DIRECTIONS
Think about the intrusive thoughts or feelings you get from Mr. O. Write them down in the first column. What are some good sarcastic comebacks you can say to him? Write those in the second column.

LET'S TALK SCIENCE
When people have OCD, their brain has a hard time accepting doubt and uncertainty. When you practice sprinkling doubt into your responses to OCD, you retrain your brain to be able to sit with discomfort, doubt and uncertainty.

When I have this intrusive thought:	I can say this to Mr. O:

IGNORING MR. O'S CHATTER

One last defense move is the power of accepting OCD thoughts without taking any action at all. As you play the OCD Game, you might get so good at handling the discomfort OCD brings that you don't need to respond at all to Mr. O.

What would this look like? Like a cloud passing you in the sky...

DIRECTIONS:

In the comic strip fill in the boxes. In Box 1, draw you doing something you love to do. In Box 2, draw you noticing an OCD thought. Fill in the cloud. In Box 3, draw yourself continuing to do the activity you love.

REAL-LIFE PRACTICE

Try this out for real! Pick an OCD thought once a day where you'll do nothing but notice it as it moves farther and farther out of your awareness. Come back and share your observations here. How did it feel to let the thoughts pass by naturally? What did you notice?

LET'S TALK SCIENCE

It is not the discomfort or worrying that grows the neural pathways of OCD. It is the compulsions you do to stop feeling anxious or uncomfortable that grow OCD. When you just notice these upsetting thoughts and feelings and do nothing to make them go away, they eventually go away on their own without you firing the neural pathways that grow your OCD stronger.

ROADMAP TO SUCCESS

Now that you have all the ninja moves, let's come up with a plan of attack. It is the **compulsions** that feed Mr. O, not the upsetting thoughts. If you can learn how to stop doing the compulsions, Mr. O will get smaller. It can help to see all the compulsions you are currently doing to grow Mr. O.

DIRECTIONS

Make a list of all the compulsions you do for OCD. Don't forget that avoidance, reassurance and mental activities like debating, counting and other mental actions are compulsions too! Once you have this list, try not to add any new compulsions to it, but if one slips in, add it to the list. Mr. O is sneaky, and the harder you work, the harder he'll work.

Use the OCD Game and your ninja levels to reduce and eventually get rid of the compulsions. As you get rid of a compulsion, come back to this list and cross it off. It will feel so good to see all those crossed-off compulsions!

EXTRA TIP

As you work to get rid of compulsions, you might find that some compulsions just go away on their own! That's good news. Don't forget to cross those other compulsions off your list as well.

COMPULSION LIST

....

....

....

....

....

REAL-LIFE PRACTICE

If you don't want to forget about this list, copy it and hang it up somewhere you can see it each day.

SECTION FOUR
OFFENSE
HOW TO BUG OCD BACK

You now know how Mr. O shows up and how he gets you to grow him. You've also developed great ninja moves to play the OCD Game and defend yourself when Mr. O comes knocking. Learning and practicing **defense** is a powerful way to squish Mr. O and make him smaller. But now adding **offense** will be the icing on the cake. Doing offense and defense together will squash Mr. O quicker than doing one or the other alone.

Offense is when you make **your move**. You aren't responding to **his** chess move. You aren't blocking **his** attempt at making a goal. You are making your own move. You are trying to score your own goal!

In this section, I will teach you offense where you purposely upset Mr. O to build your OCD muscles. It is like going to an OCD gym and lifting weights. You poke at Mr. O and then resist feeding him with compulsions. This will make you stronger.

WHAT IS ERP?

ERP is a fancy therapy term that stands for Exposure Response Prevention. What that means is you **purposely do** something Mr. O doesn't like (that is called an **exposure**) and then you resist feeding him (that is called **response prevention**). It is called response prevention because you are preventing the response Mr. O wants you to do. When you do that you shrink him smaller!

ERP can build your OCD muscles super strong so you are better able to handle it when Mr. O throws those upsetting thoughts and feelings at you! When we create an exposure, we want to ask ourselves two things:

- What thoughts or feelings does Mr. O throw at me?
- What does Mr. O want me **to do** when he gives me those thoughts?

DIRECTIONS

Write down an intrusive thought/feeling Mr. O gives you in the first column. In the second column, write down what Mr. O wants you to do when he gives you that thought or feeling. That is your compulsion.

Mr. O tells me:	Mr. O wants me to:
Example: You are a bad person because...	*Ask my mom if that's true*
Example: Are you sure that looks right?	*Fix it until it feels just right*

ACTIVITY 27
THE INGREDIENTS OF AN EXPOSURE

Creating an exposure is like making a recipe. We want to make sure you have all the ingredients in the exposure. The first step is thinking of what theme you want to focus on first. You can focus on one or two themes at a time when doing exposures. You can change what theme you are working on at any time, especially if Mr. O switches his tactics and bothers you with something new. The most important thing is that you are always targeting something.

So to start, think about what you want to work on first. This is up to you. Any weight lifting will help you build muscles to squash Mr. O.

DIRECTIONS
Use the questions below to decide what OCD theme you want to work on first.

What does Mr. O take away from you or your life that you want back? (Example: time, activities, objects you love. Refer back to Activity 10 if you need help)

....

....

EXTRA TIP
As you go, you can always change what themes and exposures you want to do, so don't worry too much about what you pick first. The most important thing is that you go to the OCD gym every day to build those OCD muscles.

Where does Mr. O bother you the most? (Example: At school, when you sleep, when you are showering, when you go to the bathroom etc.)

....

....

What thoughts or feelings does Mr. O give you when you are in those places?

....

....

What OCD theme is that most related to? (Think back to Activity 4)

....

....

What are you the most willing to tackle first based on your answers
above?

....

....

I want to work on this OCD theme:

....

My core fear or core discomfort around this theme is:

....

These are the compulsions I do around this OCD theme (don't forget
things you avoid or mental activities you do in your head):

....

....

WHAT THOUGHTS ARE IN YOUR OCD THEME?

Each OCD theme comes with lots of intrusive thoughts or feelings. We want to see what Mr. O is throwing at you so we know what ingredients to use in your exposures.

Here are a few examples of an OCD theme and some of the thoughts Mr. O uses around those themes.

OCD THEME
1. Fear of germs
2. Fear of being a bad person
3. Fear of disgust

INTRUSIVE THOUGHTS

1. Things in my house are germy. Things from school are germy. If I touch germs, I might get sick.

2. What if I'm lying? What if I cheated? If I'm bad, no one will like me.

3. If I see that, I'll feel grossed out. If I touch that, I'll feel disgusted. If I feel disgusted, I won't be able to handle the discomfort.

DIRECTIONS

Write down the one or two OCD themes you picked in the last activity.
Fill in the bowl with the thoughts Mr. O throws at you around that theme.

Developing a Menu of Exposures

Now that you know what you want to focus on, we can create a menu of exposure ideas. Exposures are exercises that purposely trigger Mr. O. The difference between an exposure and a ninja Level 4, doing the opposite, is that you do an exposure when Mr. O **isn't** bothering you. You aren't responding to Mr. O – you are waking him up and bothering **him** first.

Below are some examples of exposures based on themes. Some of these may seem scary (especially if you have one of the themes in the examples). Remember, these are just examples.

You can start off as big or as small as you want with exposures. You can do a humongous, brave exposure one day and do a smaller one the next. It is okay to mix and match the difficulty level of each exposure. The most important thing is that you do an exposure each day. When you practice building your OCD muscles each day, you get stronger and stronger.

OCD THEME: GERMS

Close your eyes and imagine touching...

FEAR OF GERMS

Put sticky notes on things around the house that say: "Are there germs on this? Maybe. Maybe not."

FEAR OF GERMS

Touch the floor and say: "I hope I get sick," and then don't wash your hands.

FEAR OF GERMS

Have your parent tell you (or text you) twice throughout the day: "You may or may not get sick!"

FEAR OF GERMS

Touch a doorknob and don't wash your hands.

FEAR OF GERMS

Let your dog lick you without washing your hands.

FEAR OF GERMS

OCD THEME: BEING BAD
(Moral OCD)

OCD THEME: DISGUST

Write a story about doing bad things and the worst thing happening. Read it each day.

FEAR OF BEING BAD

Put sticky notes on things around the house that say: "Did I lie today?"

FEAR OF BEING BAD

Role-play with your parent and say something bad. Make them have a big reaction.

FEAR OF BEING BAD

Make a funny song with the words that Mr. O says are bad.

FEAR OF BEING BAD

Make a funny picture of you doing something bad and everyone having a big reaction to it.

FEAR OF BEING BAD

Play "Two truths and a lie" where your parent has to guess which one is the lie.

FEAR OF BEING BAD

Close your eyes and imagine touching the thing that makes you feel disgusted.

FEAR OF DISGUST

Put something you find disgusting in the room with you.

FEAR OF DISGUST

Touch the thing Mr. O says is disgusting.

FEAR OF DISGUST

Look at pictures of the thing Mr. O says is disgusting.

FEAR OF DISGUST

Cut out pictures of things that are disgusting and play a memory match game with them.

FEAR OF DISGUST

Have someone touch some of your things with something that is disgusting.

FEAR OF DISGUST

DIRECTIONS

Fill out the box and bowls below with your own OCD theme(s) and exposure ideas! Remember they can be a combination of small and big exposures.

EXTRA TIP

These are just ideas. You don't have to be ready to do all of them. As you build up your muscles, the harder exposures will seem less hard. Write any ideas you have, even if you aren't quite ready to do some of them.

REMEMBER, DON'T FEED MR. O

Doing the exposures you listed in the last activity will be fantastic! But if you feed Mr. O during or after an exposure, it loses all its power. Remember ERP is doing an **Exposure** while making sure to do **Response Prevention**. That means not doing anything to get out of the discomfort the exposure may cause during or after it.

Here are just a few ways Mr. O will try to get you to undo all your hard work.

But you're too smart to let Mr. O ruin your progress!

DIRECTIONS
Write down all the things Mr. O might do to ruin your exposure. If you know what sneaky moves he'll try, you'll be less likely to fall for his traps!

When doing an exposure I won't do this:

....

....

....

....

....

....

WHAT'S ON THE MENU?

Now that you know what goes into an exposure and which areas you want to target, let's make a menu you'll use each day!

DIRECTIONS

What's cooking? Write down an exposure idea on each plate. These are exposures you are currently willing to do. Have a variety of exposures from difficult to easy.

ACTIVITY 32
SPRINKLE SOME FUN
EARN BRAVERY PRIZES

We are missing one key ingredient – the cherry on top! What's the fun of doing hard things without some prizes sprinkled in? Doing exposures can be fun, especially when you are earning things for doing them! When you do an exposure, have your parent or caregiver tell you how many points it will be worth. Exchange your bravery points for fun rewards!

DIRECTIONS
Sit down with your parent or caregiver and fill out what is in your Bravery Store!

REAL-LIFE PRACTICE
Make earning bravery points easier and more convenient by taking a chore app and converting it into an ERP rewards app!

EXTRA TIP
Don't make all the prizes too hard. In the beginning, it can help to earn prizes easily. Also, it doesn't have to be an item. It can be a privilege or an experience. Remember, it should be something you are motivated to earn!

SHOP
BEST-SELLERS

Item/privilege: **# of bravery points:**

....

....

....

....

ACTIVITY 33
LET'S DO THIS!

Now that you know how to create an exposure and how to not let Mr. O ruin one, let's get started! Here are the steps to doing an exposure.

Each day:

1. Pick an idea from the menu you created.
2. Discuss with your caregiver how many bravery points you will earn.
3. Remind yourself what compulsions you'll resist during and after the exposure.
4. Pat yourself on the back for trying something brave!

DIRECTIONS
Keep a log of what exposures you do each day! This will help you see your progress over time.

REAL-LIFE PRACTICE

Make it easier to track by making a sheet you can hang up or keep close by.

Date:	OCD theme:	Exposure:	Bravery points:

ACTIVITY 34
AVOID MR. O'S SNEAKY MOVES

Mr. O won't just sit back and let you shrink him! He will make his own sneaky moves to sabotage your success.

Here are just a few ways Mr. O might try to destroy your efforts:

- Tell you it's too hard.
- Make you do tons of compulsions later that day.
- Say you are going to make your issues worse.
- Make you find sneaky ways to get out of exposures.
- Make you create exposures that won't upset Mr. O.

DIRECTIONS

Write down some ways you think Mr. O will try to ruin your exposures. What are some ways you can outsmart his sneaky moves?

Mr. O's sneaky moves:	My sneaky counter moves:

SiLLY CReATiVe ExPOSURe IDeAS

When doing exposures, don't forget to have fun! Learn how to create creative exposures. Here are just a few ideas:

- Create a song with exposure words or topics in them.
- Make a creative video with exposure words or topics in them.
- Make a play with triggering themes and put it on for your family.
- Make a newspaper headline with your worst fear (use an app that creates fake news headlines).
- Put contaminated water in a water gun or water balloons.
- Play "Go fish" with cards you've made that have triggering pictures, words or phrases on them.
- Play a memory card game with cards you've made that have triggering pictures, words or phrases on them.

Those are just a few creative ideas!

DIRECTIONS

Think about some of the exposures you had written on your menu. Can you think of more fun, creative ways to do them? Write your ideas below.

ACTIVITY 36
LaYeRiNG EHPOSURES

As you develop your OCD muscles, you'll be able to make an exposure harder and even more effective. Start with the first-layer exposure. As that gets easy, do the first and second layers. When that gets easy, add a third layer. The last layer is often around the core fear driving your OCD theme.

Let me show you an example:

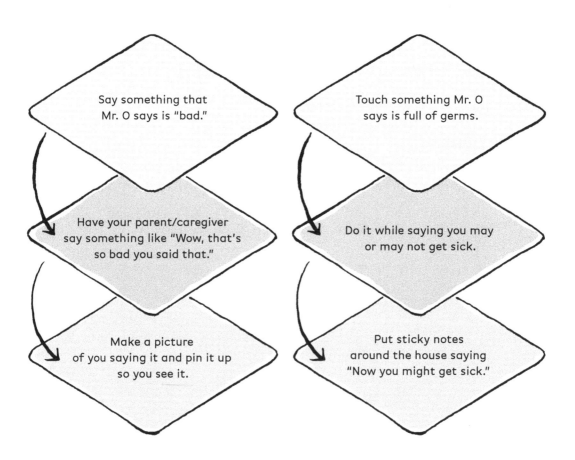

Say something that
Mr. O says is "bad."

Touch something Mr. O
says is full of germs.

Have your parent/caregiver
say something like "Wow, that's
so bad you said that."

Do it while saying you may
or may not get sick.

Make a picture
of you saying it and pin it up
so you see it.

Put sticky notes
around the house saying
"Now you might get sick."

DIRECTIONS

Now you practice. Fill in the empty squares. Start with an easy exposure and see how you can build on that exposure to make it more challenging.

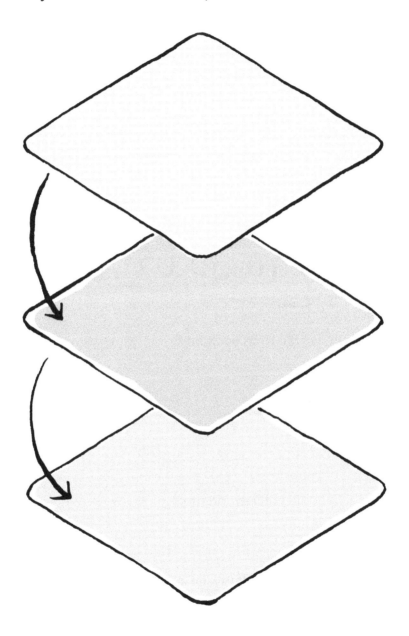

REAL-LIFE PRACTICE

Start growing your OCD muscles by doing the first layer of what you draw. When that gets easy, add the second layer. Eventually, add the final layer!

MaKiNG iT a HaBiT

Doing exposures is incredibly powerful, but only if you remember to do them. Crushing OCD is your job! Parents and caregivers can remind you, but ultimately OCD is wreaking havoc in **your** life and you are the only one who can take that power back.

DIRECTIONS

Come up with a plan for how you'll remember to do exposures each day. If it involves other people, have them complete this plan with you.

To do list

I'll do exposures at this time each day:

....

I'll remind myself by:

....

If I forget, this person will remind me:

....

If I don't want to do it, I'll tell myself this:

....

SECTION FIVE
HOOKING OTHERS IN

Mr. O doesn't want you to just grow him! He wants everyone around you to feed him too. That is why it is important to understand the many different trickster moves OCD will do to get fed. We touched on this in Activity 9 when we talked about accommodations. In this section, we'll reveal all the sneaky moves Mr. O might throw at you and how to come up with a plan to stop him in his tracks!

HOW MR. O GETS OTHERS TO FEED HIM

We talked about how Mr. O gets fed in Activity 9. We call those behaviors "accommodations" because the people around you **accommodate** Mr. O and give him what he wants. It can help to review your answers from Activity 9 before doing this activity.

Let's dig deeper and make sure Mr. O doesn't get fed by others!

DIRECTIONS

In the first column, write down the name of the person who is doing the accommodation. In the second column, write down what they do (even if they are unaware) that feeds your OCD.

EXTRA TIP

Remember that an accommodation can be anything someone does for your OCD. It can be:

- a question they answer
- something they have to say or repeat
- a thing, person or situation they help you avoid
- an action they have to take
- supplies they provide (excessive soap, toilet paper, wipes, laundry detergent, etc.).

Person:	Accommodation they do to feed my OCD:

ACCOMMODATIONS ROADMAP

Stopping accommodations from others can be hard, but you don't have to do it all at once! Remember, you can't fully squash Mr. O if others continue to feed him. Let's make a roadmap of the accommodations you want to eventually work on.

DIRECTIONS

Make a list of the accommodations others do and rate them on a 1–10 scale: 1 = it would be easy if they stopped doing the accommodation all the way up to 10 = it would be super hard if they stopped doing it.

EXTRA TIP

Be as specific as possible and list all of them. You won't have to work on all of them at once!

Person(s) doing accommodation:	Accommodation:	Scale rating:

REAL-LIFE PRACTICE

You'll probably forget some accommodations! Spend a few days paying attention to how Mr. O involves others. When you notice a new thing, come back and add it to this list. The more complete this list is, the better!

ACTIVITY 40
REMOVING ACCOMMODATIONS TO CRUSH MR. O

Now that you have a list of all the accommodations Mr. O has people do, let's come up with a plan to stop him!

DIRECTIONS

Take one accommodation from the list in Activity 39 to work on first. Fill in the questions below.

We will remove this accommodation:

....

....

Instead of asking this person for this accommodation, I'll do this instead:

....

....

If I ask this person to do this accommodation, they will respond with:

....

....

EXTRA TIP

Here are some helpful responses your loved ones can say if you ask them to do or respond to an accommodation:

- I'm sorry Mr. O is bugging you.
- I love you, so I won't grow Mr. O.
- Sounds like Mr. O is trying to talk to me.
- Tell Mr. O I love you and won't answer that.

Reassurance Cards
A HELPFUL TOOL

One of the biggest accommodations is reassurance. Reassurance will look different depending on your theme.

You might ask for people to give you reassurance:

- if food is okay to eat
- if you are a good person
- if you did something wrong
- if something is clean
- if someone touched something
- if something is safe
- if you'll get sick
- if they accept your apology.

Those are only a few examples! It can be anything that OCD demands you know. When you get reassurance, it makes Mr. O want more and more reassurance.

Let's talk about how you can cut down on reassurance.

DIRECTIONS

Cut out little squares that you will use as reassurance cards. You can photocopy or make as many as you need (examples: "I am going to feed Mr. O," "Mr. O wants a snack" or just a simple "Reassurance Card"). Write a silly or motivating message on each card. Fill in the blanks below each day:

I will receive .... reassurance cards today.

If I don't use all my reassurance cards, I will earn: ....

If I ask for reassurance after I use all my cards, my loved one will not provide me with reassurance and will respond this way:

....

....

....

....

Here is an example of what your reassurance card can look like:

REAL-LIFE PRACTICE

Be consistent and do this every day! Pick a lower number of cards each day as you build your OCD muscles to handle the discomfort! Before you know it, you won't be needing reassurance as much!

ACTIVITY 42
WORK YOUR WAY DOWN THE LIST!

The goal is to eventually remove all the accommodations from your list. Accommodations are just compulsions that involve other people. The only way to squash Mr. O is to get rid of all compulsions, including the ones other people are participating in!

DIRECTIONS

Take the list of accommodations from Activity 39 and write them all down below. Work on removing one accommodation at a time by using the worksheet in Activity 40 for each new accommodation you focus on. Come back to this activity and cross off the accommodation when you've completely got rid of it. Don't forget to do a happy dance before moving on to the next accommodation! Keep going until everything on this list is crossed off.

EXTRA TIP
Don't forget to make it fun. Adding bravery points and prizes for not needing accommodations can be a great way to motivate you and celebrate your brave efforts!

MR. O HAS A MELTDOWN

When Mr. O doesn't get what he wants, he can sometimes have a meltdown. He might fill you with fear and anger. It is normal to have these strong emotions. You might want to lash out and demand that people feed Mr. O. You might even insist it isn't Mr. O at all.

It can help to have a plan in place on how you want to handle these strong feelings.

DIRECTIONS:

Fill in the blanks below. Write down your plan on a piece of paper that you can hang up and see easily when you are upset.

Mr. O can make me mad when:

....

....

....

When I'm feeling frustrated, the best thing to say to me is:

....

....

....

These are the things that calm me down:

....

....

....

These are the things you can do to calm me down:

....

....

....

SECTION SIX
YOU ARE
AWESOME!

Squashing Mr. O can be an up-and-down battle. In this section, we are going to talk about how to handle the bumps while remembering how amazing you are!

ACTIVITY 44
CELEBRATE YOUR SMALL WINS!

Shrinking Mr. O can be challenging at times, and you might get too hard on yourself. It is important to remember that sometimes you'll be crushing it and sometimes it might crush you. That is part of the process. All your small wins will lead to big success in the end.

EXTRA TIP

There is always a win, even when you are struggling. What is one thing you did today that Mr. O wouldn't want you to do? What is one brave action you took? Remember, even the smallest steps should be celebrated. If you are stuck, ask those around you what they noticed.

DIRECTIONS

Create a journal where you celebrate your small wins every day! Make a journal entry below each day.

Date:	Win for the day:

REAL-LIFE PRACTICE

Take this celebration to the next level! Get a whiteboard and write your wins on it each day. Maybe your loved ones can add things they notice. Put it in a place where you can see it.

CRUSHING OCD WORKBOOK FOR KIDS

KEEP UP THE GOOD WORK

Shrinking Mr. O is a marathon, not a sprint. It takes time and strength. There might be days when it feels too hard. There might even be times when you want to give up and just let Mr. O have what he wants. Let's give you some words of hope during those times!

DIRECTIONS
Draw a picture that will help you when you feel like giving up. Add uplifting words around the picture that you can read when feeling discouraged.

REAL-LIFE PRACTICE
Make a video that you can watch when you are feeling down. What would you want to remind yourself? How would you cheer up your future self? Keep the recording and watch it whenever you are feeling discouraged. Update the video from time to time to keep it fresh.

I AM...

Having OCD can be hard, but it can be even harder when it makes you feel bad about yourself. Some of the strongest, bravest kids have OCD, and you are one of them. Do an activity to remind yourself of that!

Here are some examples:

- Mr. O says I am bad. But really, I am a kind, thoughtful person.
- Mr. O says I am weak. But really, I am a strong, powerful person.

DIRECTIONS
Fill in the blanks below. Draw a picture of yourself with all your wonderful traits in the frame.

Mr. O says I am:	But really, I am:

SECTION SEVEN
KEEPING UP YOUR
SUCCESS

Shrinking Mr. O isn't about getting to a finish line. It is about keeping him small. Once you successfully crush your OCD and make Mr. O so super tiny you can barely hear him, you want to keep it that way! This last section will give you important tools to keep up all your hard work.

I'VE GOT MY EYE ON YOU, MR. O

Always keep your eye out for new ways Mr. O is trying to grow bigger again. Mr. O will be waiting, looking for an opportunity to grow, but the good news is all the skills you've learned will easily shrink him back down. The important thing is that you catch his sneaky moves before he grows too big again.

Let's talk about how to do that!

EXTRA TIP

Mr. O might try to sneak in a whole new type of theme that you might miss! If you understand how **all** of OCD works, you won't miss even these new sneaky themes.

DIRECTIONS:

Fill in the answers below. Turn the page upside down to see the correct responses.

1. OCD starts with an intrusive ....

2. Mr. O will then want me to .... or .... something to get some brief relief.

3. But the more I .... or .... the bigger it grows.

4. OCD can be about any ....

5. Here are a few OCD themes (if you get stuck go back to Activity 4 where we talk about themes):

....

....

....

....

....

ANSWERS

1. Intrusive thought or feeling
2. Do or avoid
3. Do or avoid
4. Theme
5. Moral, symmetry, contamination, just right, emetophobia (fear of throwing up), harm, existential, sensorimotor

An Exposure a Day Keeps OCD at Bay

It can be very easy to stop doing exposures because Mr. O isn't bothering you anymore. But it is **so** important to keep those OCD muscles strong. Even if exposures aren't stressful or hard, it is important to keep up the good work.

Let's make a plan so you don't lose all the progress you are making!

DIRECTIONS

Answer the questions below to create a schedule to continue doing exposures. Don't worry if the exposures are super easy now!

EXTRA TIP

Remember to keep changing the exposures. If you see a new OCD theme popping up, switch your exposures to crush the new theme. It is normal to have to crush new themes as you make progress.

What is the OCD theme that was the strongest and most difficult for you?

....

What are some intrusive thoughts you had around that theme?

....

What are some compulsions you had to do?

....

What are some creative exposures you can do? Write down five of them:

1. ....

2. ....

3. ....

4. ....

5. ....

When will you do an exposure?

....

What will you earn for doing an exposure? (Yes, having fun and earning bravery points should still be part of the deal.)

....

ACTIVITY 49
DON'T FALL FOR THESE SNEAKY TRAPS

Mr. O doesn't give up easily. He might find ways to try to sabotage your progress. But if you know his sneaky moves, you won't fall for them!

Here are a few he might try to pull:

- Make you keep any new intrusive thoughts or feelings a secret.
- Make you feel like maybe you never had OCD at all.
- Make you feel like you are done with OCD and you don't need to look out for new issues.
- Make you feel like OCD was keeping you safe.

Those are just a few!

DIRECTIONS

Draw a picture of what Mr. O might tell you in order to sabotage your progress. Draw a picture of how you will handle it when he does!

IT'S TIME TO CELEBRATE

Congratulations! You did some amazing work to get to the end of this workbook! It is so helpful to take time to celebrate all your successes and this is one of them!

DIRECTIONS
How will you celebrate all the hard work you did in this book to crush Mr. O? OCD is hard, and celebrating all your wins is super important. Fill in the answers below.

I've done brave things while going through this book including:

....

....

....

....

I am proud of myself because:

....

....

....

....

This is how I will celebrate the hard work I put into this workbook:

....

....

....

....

ADDiTiONAL ReSOURCeS

AT Parenting Survival School
Natasha Daniels offers in-depth, on-demand, online video courses on anxiety and OCD for parents, kids and teens.

AT Parenting Survival: Support for Parents Raising Kids with Anxiety and OCD
Website full of resources for parents raising kids with anxiety and/or OCD.
www.ATparentingsurvival.com

AT Parenting Community: Online Membership for Parents Raising Kids with Anxiety or OCD
Get ongoing support from Natasha Daniels and other parents through weekly live Zoom classes, monthly support group calls and ongoing resources.
www.ATparentingcommunity.com

Natasha Daniels YouTube channel
Weekly YouTube videos for kids and teens on topics related to anxiety and OCD.
www.youtube.com/@Natashadanielsocdtherapist

Natasha Daniels Podcast: AT Parenting Survival Podcast
Weekly podcast episodes to help parents raising kids with anxiety or OCD.

DR DAWN'S MINI BOOKS ABOUT MIGHT FEARS

Dawn Huebner, PhD · *Illustrated by Liza Stevens*

Helping children ages 6–10 live happier lives.

Facing Mighty Fears About Animals

ISBN 978 1 78775 946 6
eISBN 978 1 78775 947 3

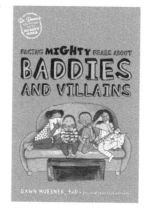

Facing Mighty Fears About Baddies and Villains

ISBN 978 1 83997 462 5
eISBN 978 1 83997 463 2

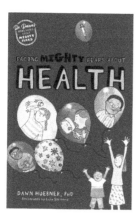

Facing Mighty Fears About Health

ISBN 978 1 78775 928 2
eISBN 978 1 78775 927 5

Facing Mighty Fears About Trying New Things

ISBN 978 1 78775 950 3
eISBN 978 1 78775 951 0

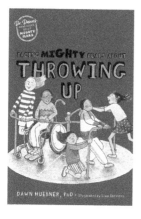

Facing Might Fears About Throwing Up

ISBN 978 1 78775 925 1
eISBN 978 1 78775 926 8

Facing Mighty Fears About Making Mistakes

ISBN 978 1 83997 466 3
eISBN 978 1 83997 467 0

Watch out for future titles in the Dr. Dawn's Mini Books About Mighty Fears series.

THE HEALTHY COPING COLOURING BOOK AND JOURNAL

Creative Activities to Help Manage Stress, Anxiety and Other Big Feelings

Pooky Knightsmith
Illustrated by Emily Hamilton

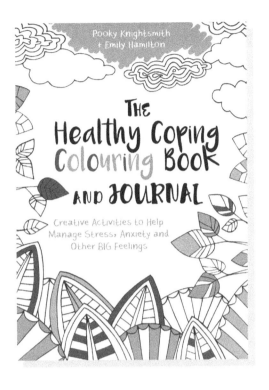

Packed full of creative activities and coping strategies, this journal and colouring book is the perfect companion when faced with difficult thoughts and feelings.

Whether you are stressed out at home or school, feeling anxious or simply in need of some relaxation, this workbook provides a place for you to express your emotions.

Put your own personal stamp on colouring, journaling and drawing activities and explore healthy ways of coping with difficult feelings such as anger and anxiety through inspirational quotes, poems and practical advice.

With a range of activities that introduce mindfulness and encourage relaxation, this workbook will help young people aged 8–14 to develop the tools needed to prepare for and respond to future difficult situations. It is also an invaluable resource for parents and carers, teachers, counsellors and psychologists to use with young people in their care.

£10.99 | $18.95 | PB | 208PP | ISBN 978 1 78592 139 1 | eISBN 978 1 78450 405 2

STAND UP TO OCD

A CBT Self-Help Guide and Workbook for Teens

Kelly Wood and Douglas Fletcher

Imagine each person's brain has a captain and crew. For a person struggling with OCD, it's as if OCD has kidnapped the captain and changed the settings in the brain. Luckily, there are plenty of tips and skills you can learn to disobey OCD and not do what he tells you.

Join David, Riya and Sarah as they find out about how OCD sneaks into their lives and all the tricks you can use to stand up to OCD!

This illustrated CBT self-help guide and workbook is ideal for young people with OCD aged 12–17. It gives teens a deeper understanding of how OCD works and how they can carry out their own CBT with the help of the interactive workbook at the back of the book.

£14.99 | $21.95 | PB | 164PP | ISBN 978 1 78592 835 2 | eISBN 978 1 78450 973 6

TOUCH AND GO JOE

A Teen's Experience of OCD

Joe Wells

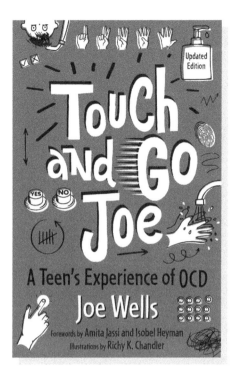

In this down-to-earth, fun and empowering book, Joe Wells talks about his teenage experience of OCD and all the coping mechanisms and treatment options that have worked for him.

It's packed full of brilliant, honest advice for others struggling with this disorder, written by someone who understands what it's like to be a teen with OCD.

This updated edition with all-new illustrations includes a brand-new chapter written 16 years later, detailing how Joe overcame his disorder and is now a successful comedian.

£12.99 | $19.95 | PB | 160PP | ISBN 978 1 78775 777 6 | eISBN 978 1 78775 778 3

NOTES